heather leigh

ISBN (paperback): 978-1-7774708-0-7
ISBN (ebook): 978-1-7774708-1-4

All interior illustrations done by Francesca Adani
Cover Design by Anamaria Stefan
Page Design and Typesetting by Paul Baillie-Lane

Contents

I dedicate this to my late mother,
Barbara Joy Milligan.

Rage

It fills you
With boundless fire
Leaves behind nothing
But embers of a forbidden flame
Chokes you
With foul decay
Burns your eyes with tears
Blurry vision and smoke-filled hopes
Coats your lungs with battered charcoal
Leaving you
With tattered wounds
Rage;
The fire starts small
But don’t let it go
Uncontrolled
You will be left
With nothing but dust-filled fragments of debris.

November

When I am sad, I do not cry
I howl
When I am happy, I do not smile
I form into a ball of pure bliss
When I am angry, I do not yell
I ignite
Oh, but when I love, I do not just appreciate
I blossom a growing garden
That thrives on the good in all individuals
But feeling so deeply is not always so great
Because when I am heartbroken, I do not simply sorrow
I drown.

Nowhere

No one knows
What goes on inside my head
Second guessing every move
No one knows
The thoughts that submerge my brain
There is malignancy
And it is starting to spread
I feel I do not belong
Anywhere.

Be The Lion In A Herd Of Sheep

Society
Hair a jumble of blonde strands
Chaotic to a world of perfection
A face marked with scars of red spots
Oozing with insecurity
The height of small hopes and vast dreams
Too tall to reach
Four eyes are better than two, Mom used to say
No
Four eyes reflect the desperation
When words shatter
The glass protecting your vision
Lips chapped in winter's chill
Wishing you could look like the girl that sits in the back of the class
Trying to change
For others' approval

All because
Society engraved perfection
Into a vulnerable mind.

You Equals Me In This Battle Against Myself

You have beaten my brain
With the perception that I will never be enough
Your fingerprints have now
Bruised the walls of my skull
Whispers rattle the unstable frame
That is only built on apprehensions
Your voice has burrowed its way through my veins
Bleeding your pain into my heart
Your misery has turned into my shadow
Stitching the two together so sadness seeps through my wounds
You have conquered
You as in me
As in myself
You as in I.

Camouflage

Somedays the air gets entangled between my lungs
It constricts my heart to only beating at a melancholy flutter
My thoughts suffocate my mentality
And my vision gets blurred to a shade of misery
I feel myself diminishing with no one to hold onto
I do not want to burden
The people that confide in me
My mind buries me in rubble
With no way to set myself free
So why do I not just disappear
Maybe then the air can extricate from my lungs
And my thoughts can relieve my mind of despair
I won't have to worry
If I just become the wind that tremors the trees
Instead of being the whirlwind
That lives inside my mind.

Clarity

Why is happiness so hard to uncover?
We search our whole lives
To be fulfilled with pure bliss
While we pursue some sort of expectation
Of how things are supposed to be
We miss out
On every little thing that happiness is made from.

Fast Forward

She rushed through life
Trying to reach the final goal
Drawn by a daydream
The scenario playing within her head
She raced past all the countless moments
The laughter and the memories
When she finally reached that expectation
She only wished
She could go back to the beginning
And appreciate the moments that she left behind.

Why Is It So Hard To Love?

The world screams with solitude when I do not love
But falls silent
Hushed with agony
When I do.

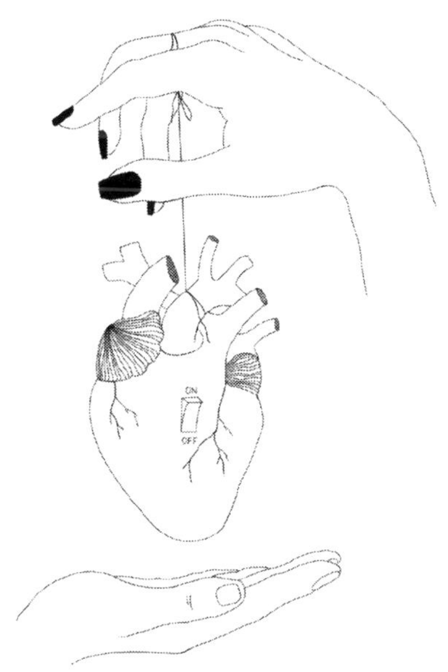

Goodbyes

The day you left
Was the day I realized
I hadn't stopped thinking about you
Since the moment we met.

Out Of Reach

Happiness exists within our fingertips
Surges through our veins
But most days
It is just a little too far away to grasp onto.

What Made Him So Good?

Your mind is saturated with his deception
Tire marks scraped across your deflated heart
As he raced out of your life and into another's
Yearning for closure
Replaced with defeat
He left fragments of agony carved in your soul
So why do you still miss him?

Nothingness

She’s not at the point
Where tears still stream down her face
Instead her body just trembles
Her heart just beats in anguish
And she tries with everything she can
Not to think about you
Because then at least
She doesn’t feel
Anything at all.

Addictive

He lures her with his intoxicated eyes
Swallowing her heart
Drowning her airway with lust;
Just one more sip.

Trapped By His Allure

Stale glass waves shatter
Against the wooden deck
Salt-filled mist blinds the sails
Her vision unrecognizable
Her lungs fill with grains of sand
You lure her
With your lullabies of lies
Trapping her
When she believes she is drowning in paradise
You display her like a vintage ship
Glued inside a bottle
She is bewildered by the beauty of the bottle
She doesn't see the cage you have built her
To lay to rest in.

Drenched In You

What if I can't
Wash you off my skin
No matter how many times
I drench myself in boiling water?

What if I can't
Remove the scent of you from my bedsheets
No matter how many new sets I buy?

What if you leave
And forget all about me
And no matter how hard I try
I cannot
Forget you?

The One Who Got Away

She let him go
Afraid that he would cause her heart too much pain
But letting him go was more painful
Than a shattered heart
Could ever be.

August

Did one night with her
mean more to you
than a lifetime with me?

Did you like the way
her eyes shone in the sun
better than you liked mine?

Did your name sound better
dripping from her lips?

Did you think about me
at all
as your lips glided on the nape of her neck?

Did you consider
the tears drenching my face
when you told her
her blue eyes reminded you of your favourite summer's day?

Was she fun because she was new?

Was her bra pink
like my favourite colour
or black
like the colour my heart started to turn?

You knew what you were doing

So I hope you fell in love
with the way her hair washes down her back
the way her figure is shaped.

Did your friends applaud you
congratulate you
even though you knew what you were doing was wrong?

I hope you fell in love with her
the way I fell in love with you.

And I hope she shatters your heart
like you shattered mine.

And I hope she walks out of your life
like I am walking out of yours.

Cemented Inside Of Me

I don't know
What it is about you
The way your eyes flicker gold stars
Or the way your voice
Makes up the waves of the ocean
Memories emerge
When you interrupt my dreams
Yet you drenched someone else in happiness
And that makes me miss you more.

Peeling Away Her Humanity

If you truly want
I can drape her skin over mine
I can pull my teeth out and replace them with hers
I can shave my head bald
And wear her hair as my crown
I can wear her eyes as pearls smothering my neck
I could wear her lips
So enhanced with secrets there is no room for air to reach
my lungs
I could reform myself into her
Because then, I would be her
And that is what you truly want
Never me
Only,
Her.

We Are Not The Same

I replay your betrayal so much in my mind
It has knit itself within the veins of my beating heart
I replay the apology
That never dripped from your lips
I bleed the tears that never fell from your eyes
And hold my own trembling body
While your hands hold your bruised ego
I am shattered
While you merely pretend to be broken.

She Was Your Saviour, Now You Cannot Be Saved

She was home
She was the walls that could have protected you
The stain-glass windows
That could have brightened your future
The temple carved from love
Even though she was just an average girl
Her home could have helped you grow
Instead you chose a faraway castle
The beauty slithers amongst the exterior
But is decaying from its foundation
With nothing to give
Because it has all rotted away
You chose her
When you already had a home.

Tongue-Tied

He made her feel so wanted, yet so undesirable, within the same sentence.

Blindsided

Deceit dripped off your tongue
Smoldering her skin
If only her skin could repel
Your hollow phrases
And her heart could shield itself
From the carnage you were about to enact
You begged her not to leave
Yet you were the one that vanished into another's arms
That weren't quite her own
Empty intentions sunk into her heart
Blindsided by the one she adores
Never able to trust another word
That splashes her tender heart

Memories drown her soul
Although she knows they will not bring you back
Because you moved on
And she deserves to be splashed with love instead of mendacity
Dripped with devotion that caresses her frail flesh
She deserves better than to be blindsided
By someone as delusive as you.

Can You Have Love Without Lust?

Lust will never take love's place
And until you completely understand this
You will never find the love you deserve.

Your Loss, Her Blessing

You lost pieces of her
The second you chose
Another girl
To lie amongst the sheets with
Draped in lust
Hung by remorse
The second it was over

You lost her
The moment you forgot about her.

Take My Mind For A Ride

Take me on the carousel
Spin me until I can no longer see who you truly are
Blurred lights
Blurred lies
Dizzying my thoughts with false promises
Now leave me here at this carousel alone;
I have already lost grip on reality
And we spun out of control long ago.

11:11

Do you ever think of me
The same way I think of you.

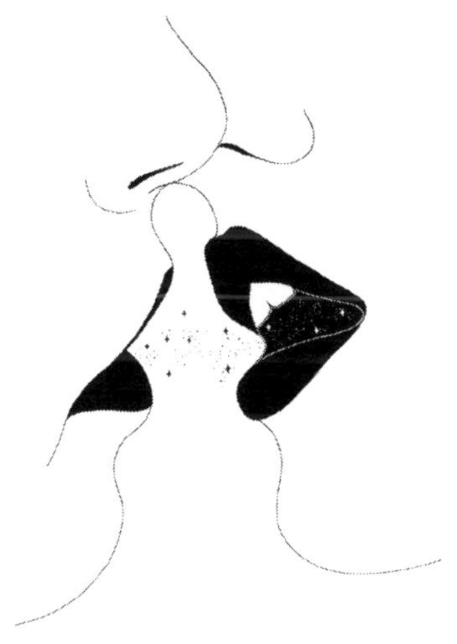

Lips Of A Deceiver

Your fragmented promises
Encircled her neck
Suffocating her
From the glistening air
Your hollow perception of needing her
Was all just part of your illusive objective
Deception grew from your lips
And she fell
For those delicate lips
Even the most trustless phrase
Could be formed into the most beautiful one
When they came from lips like yours
Lips that deceived her.

Power

How is it possible
That one individual
Can hold onto all your happiness
And control all of your vulnerabilities?

Happily Never After

I wanted to hold your hand
Touch your face
Kiss your delicate lips
Curve my body around yours
Embrace you in a feeling
Cling onto our memories
But instead I smiled and pretended
You were only a friend.

Cactus Club

You're a prick
Yet I keep coming back to get punctured.

Inadequate

The least you could have done for me
Was fight to keep me around
But you couldn't even do that.

I Breathe Dullness

I become boring
Used up
Until there is nothing left to be exploited
Constant
Like water dripping from a corroded faucet
Each drop making the same dull spatter as it hits the surface
You become bored
Of the way I cannot catch my breath
(my laugh comes from deep within,
Where my untold stories wallow in the darkness)
You become bored
With my sarcasm
(I only use my sarcasm because I am too scared to open up
I shelter the fact that my heart is fragile)
Broken beyond repair
Like a dish knocked off the counter
I watch as everyone defers to another to pick up the broken pieces
Unable to handle a little scratch
From the shattered glass
I used sarcasm
To open up to someone
Who quickly became uninterested in my beauty
I exposed my wounds

That I'd just finished stitching together
Because I thought you'd be the one to help kiss them shut

But you become bored
Of the way my eyes glistened like twinkling stars
That dance over the gloomy night sky
Every time I look at you
I bore the people who excite me the most
And that is why everyone leaves at some point.

The Chase

I know you're bad for me
And I think that makes me want you even more.

Harsh Reality

How do you tell someone you love them
When they may love someone new
Someone that is not you?

Distractions

She chases after everyone else's pain
So she doesn't have to feel her own
That is why she dates the broken:
She hopes to repair their open wounds
So she won't have to face her own.

Strength Becomes Instability

I have grown to see and believe
The good in everyone
And that is my biggest weakness.

Dynamite

Even though I am playing with fire
I pray that in the end
My heart won't get burned.

Was It Truly A Mistake?

I took a rusted shovel and dug my own grave
Burying myself alive
My own tombstone read:

To my dearly departed
You have mistaken death's breath for love.

Play Date

Women should not be scared to walk
Amidst the darkness
We don't want to rely on someone else
For our safety
Individuals should not have to grasp
A key between their fragile fingertips
For a sense of security
From the monsters that come out to play
When the streetlights turn dim
And the sun hides from the moon.

Prey

She is wearing
Black laced underwear;
Underneath
Is the skin that wraps itself around her thoughts
Like a bandage on an open wound
When wet, easily able to slide off
Unable to take the pain with it.

But you only see
The black laced underwear
Cuddling the curves of her hip bones.

(You don't see the
stories that leave scars
on her right thigh.
Or that when you slip them off
with your uncultivated fingers
you choke the oxygen
out of her)
You don't just take off that pretty
Black laced underwear.

You steal an extra layer
Fragile and unwanted
Forgotten
But you won't forget
About that pretty pair

Of underwear
That smothers the inside of her thighs
Like you forgot about the only word that could escape her mouth.
NO.

Truth Or Dare

We live in a generation where you either play the game or
get played
Boys open your legs
Before they think to open a door for you
String you along like a marionette and wrap you around
their fingertips
Bound so tight, you have no other option but to move like
a porcelain puppet
Boys play with your emotions
More than they play with themselves
They keep you waiting, and waiting and waiting
With bullshit lies that are exposed through their lucid eyes
But you cannot see how poisonous their empty promises
And vacant assurances are
Because they will smother you with such bliss
You are unable to breathe in the unspoken slanders
Boys will play you
Before you realize you are just a pawn
In the middle of their chess game
And throw you away
As if your existence
Were merely a move to reach their queen.

Damaged

The breath of a liar
Rattles the carcass of a bare tree
Sending shivers through the soil
And drowning the roots in deception
The breath of a liar
Destroys the heart
Leaving it to disintegrate.

Affliction

Sometimes she gives too much of herself away;
This can be a blessing and gift
Or a tragedy that leaves her with nothing left to grip.

The World Has Spoken

Why are you living your life waiting for him to come back?
Even the night's soft breeze
And the steady traffic
That flutters the morning routine
Knows he is not coming back to you.

Just Another Number

They either want my heart
For a short time
Or my body
Whenever it is convenient for them
But no one wants my soul or my mind
For a long time
And I think that's what hurts the most.

Piece By Piece

She thought she could heal his broken pieces
Fit them back together
In hopes to heal her own shattered parts
Instead he just took each piece of her
And tore them even more than before.

I Gave Too Much Of Myself

Weary of giving remnants of my heart
That will never come back
I am now left with gaping holes
And a heart filled with cracks.

Devil On Your Shoulder

You could have had anyone
But you chose the one who is not into you
And that in itself
Is living in hell.

Nothing Left Of Me

I gave too much away
Too much of my heart heart
To the undesired
My heart has come undone
Like a shoelace unraveling
With no one but myself noticing
Stepped on
Wearing away until it is nothing but frayed strings
Holding on by filaments of shattered hopes
My heart is becoming absently abandoned
Now I am nothing but fragments of what was once
A beating tenderness
Slipping through my shaky fingers
Struggling to find something
To mend it back together
Before I give all of myself away
And I am left with nothing
But a pit of cold obscurity replacing
The one tightly-tied shoelace I called my heart.

Hate The L Word

How can love
Make you feel so unwanted
Make your heart shatter
Stain your pillowcases
With what ifs, and what could've beens
Mark your porcelain skin
With beads of tears
Like an unfinished painting left to accrue dust?

How can love
Make you give second chances that are taken for granted
Show you that most people's colours
Are not blue or green
But shades of grey
That shadow over your own canvas of colour?

How can love
Blind you from authenticity
Make you believe
Someone will change back into the person they once
Were?

How can love
Cloud your vision with beauty and words
Words wrapped around your heart
Tugging so hard you believe it may explode?

Love lifts you so high
Just to one day watch you crumble.

How can love
Make you believe in happy endings
When there is no happiness to any end?

* * *

How can love
Make you feel so desired
Pump your heart with oxygen
To see colours in such a cruel world
Make you smile until your cheeks burst?

How can love
Make you forget
Forget your tear-stained pillow
Forget the way love once made you bleed?

How can love
Make butterflies form in the pit of your stomach
The type of butterflies you never
Want to disappear
Flourishing on the tender touch
Of skin to skin
Making your body glow
Like the sun shining through your translucent flesh?

How can love
Make you break
Yet we all thrive for that ache?

Because feeling the pain of love
Is better
Than feeling nothing at all.

Translucent

I wish you thought of me
When drunk thoughts erase sober words
When you can't fall asleep and the silence slithers around you

I wish you thought of me
A 5 p.m. when the leaves crunch under your feet
Or when the chilled air takes your breath away

I wish you thought of me
Just once
Because I think of you
Even when I cannot think for myself.

Mistrustful Beauty

Envy seeped
Within her bones
Slowly eroding the entirety of her skeleton
Latching onto her thoughts
Until they dripped with spite
And her gentle blue eyes began to flicker
Into a green shade of monster.

Fading

You are not her world
Anymore
Just a mere remnant of a time
She tries not to remember.

March 24th

Like a thunderstorm
Unexpected and piercing
With unexplained intentions
You were gone, and it couldn't have been real
It had to be a figment of my imagination
A nightmare
I couldn't force my eyes to open
I believed your chest would start to rise and fall
Like a rhythmic beat to unspoken music
You would open your eyes just like I wish I could open
mine
But you never did
Your chest did not rise
Nor lower
But stayed still just like the way my body felt
Underneath the incredulous sinking feeling
That I would not wake from this dream
Maybe if I cried a little harder
Prayed a little longer
Told you I loved you just one more time
You would come back
But you won't
Disbelief is like a rollercoaster
You wish you could get off
The highs are so high and the lows submerge you
Shaking your body until your head starts to hurt and
You just beg to get off

But there is no way to get off
So you just ride it out
And hope to god it slows down.

March 24th II

She felt bad for feeling great
Because you cannot even see the blue skies
Or the green grass anymore
Or the way the birds hum to each other
When the clouds sprinkle rain dust
On the cracked cement
She felt bad for feeling great
Because you are gone
Never again to breathe the scent of summer.

Numb

Lovely silence brushes over me
Like the world stopped moving;
Nothing felt real
It started with my feet
Prickles rushing through my veins
And then nothing.

I could not feel my legs, nor my arms, nor the tips of my fingers
All the blood
Escaped my body
Engulfing my heart and soul;
I felt empty
Staring at the floor when my knees gave out.

I could not feel myself
Hit the ground-
Becoming stone cold
Like a marble statue
My mind impaired;
Emotions not even there
I just sat and stared.

I didn't even dare
To try and get up

I knew in the moment
My whole being would collapse
In pure shock.

The world was a howling silence
And I became numb.

Soft Touch

No one can see
The loneliness that hinders behind your eyes
The darkness that slithers
Through every brain cell
Caressing every thought
Until she believes she is alone
With no one
But her own dangerous speculations.

Over And Over And Over

In the end
I break my own heart
By choosing the people that hurt me the most
Knowing they are dangerous for my heart
But thriving on the rush.

In the end
I break my own heart
And I don’t know how to stitch it
Back together again.

Sometimes What We Think Will Help Us Ends Up Hurting More

She tried to build cement barriers to block out pain
Instead she assembled a fortress
With no room to breathe
No chambers allocated for love
Suffocating her heart all on its own;
Rather than blocking out the pain
She became it.

Help Yourself First

The whispers of my enemy mesmerize my silence
Carving hatred into my memories
Tainting my breath with revulsion
Straining my heart to flutter joy
And polluting my airways
With self-doubt and apprehension
I cannot desert my enemy
As she is my lover
My biggest supporter
She is all I have
And I am her;

I am my own worst enemy.

Blackout

She is done
With the mind games -
One day you make her feel like she is
The most beautiful creation
You have ever laid eyes on
But the next day she is nothing but another person
Who blends into the crowded room
She is done
With the 3 a.m. drunken moments
When you are too intoxicated
To recollect the way your words
Bloomed into something unforgettable to her
Where your eyes meet hers
And she believes she meant something
Anything
To you
When you would caress her lips with yours
And engulf her in your soul
She is done
Believing you care about her as much as she cares about you
Because when 3 in the afternoon hits
And you are not drunk
She is just a reflection
Of a night you don't remember
You don't bother to talk to her
You act like you don't know her

Until 3 in the morning
And the darkness again hits you
And your words again blur
And you decide she means the world to you
But she is finally done.

Poetry Has Become My Bible

Poetry is not just words
Melting onto a page
It is a path to escape the pain
Of your past, present or future
Poetry connects all individuals
With the voice of words
The bond of each other
And the encouragement
That tomorrow will be better.

Manifestation

She wished for happiness
And suddenly
You appeared.

June

The sun kissed his cheek
The breath of summer melting onto his skin
He grazed the palm of my hand
My lungs filling with the promise of forever
And our future
Began to seep from the clouds above.

Seasons Change

Winter;
When bare tree branches are perched coldly
Peeled
Vulnerable and raw
The way he found her.

Fall;
When leaves tumble off the branches
Softly
Quietly
Gracefully
The way she fell for him.

Relearn, Relive, Reconnect

I want to get to know you again
Start fresh
Do things with you
Explore
Travel each other's bodies again
Our minds
(and possibly the world)
I want to relearn your habits
Your secrets
Feelings and dreams
I want to create new memories
And relive the old
I want to get to know you all over again
Like two strangers meeting
But with a history between two hearts.

Delicacy

He opened her heart
To a world filled with wanderlust
When her eyes pierced his
Her battles deep within
Tarnished into remnants of unforeseen beauty
She breathed in his unspoken fidelity
Like he was the oxygen
She needed to fill her frail lungs
He was not a craving for her anymore
He was a weakness.

My Love

Planets flutter from our skin
Stars trickling down our throats
I am a universe of darkness
And you have filled me with your stardust.

Forgotten Forever

He has kissed me so much
I've forgotten the taste of your lips
Your fingers no longer caress my skin
You no longer grasp my heart
Or linger amongst my mind
I've shed the pieces I still had left of you
And now you are no longer part of me.

Winter Wonderland

Her skin glistens
Like a soft snowflake on a brisk night
She has become ice kissed
As soon as his tender lips touch hers
She was once a scorching summer's day
Until she met him
And now he has turned her veins into glaciers
And her heart into dry ice.

Digging Up The Dirt

Loving you is my dirty little secret
In the dark places within my heart
No one needs to uncover the truth
Although loving you is slowly killing me
Driving me crazy
Burning through my veins
But this secret
Is worth the anguish
You are worth the anguish.

Copper Or Gold?

You rusted the back of her throat
Turning copper into mold
But he grows stars in her galaxy
Turning mold into sheets of gold.

Prosperous

Did you want to see me crumble
Weakened like the ruins of ancient buildings
Barely holding onto the foundation beneath me?

Did you want to see my shoulders drape low
Hanging like curtains
Keeping the sunlight from finding its way inside?

Did you want to see my eyes fill with tears
Creating waterfalls down my tender skin
Soaking into the seams of my pillowcase
And marking my sheets
With droplets of hateful love?

You may shoot me with your hollow promises
Carve me with your meaningless apologies
Your words may drown me in ice water
Thinking that if they drip with sweet lies
I won't leave you forgotten

You may kill me with your unknowing
And slaughter me with time wasted
But like ice breath on a winter's chilled day
I will rise, higher than the feeling of doubt

That you etched into my skin;

You cannot break me anymore because
I will rise up from a past that is rooted in pain.

Do Not Dull Yourself Down For Him

When he becomes lonesome
Like the moon without the company of its stars
And she cannot dull herself down
To mold into the bare sculpture he yearns for
He will move on to paint another's skin
Leaving her vividness behind
As she had too much brilliance
For him to configure into his own shallow clone.

She Is Carved From Gold

Let her words weep down your throat
Let her lips melt into droplets of honey
Collect jars of her glass tears
And alter them into stardust
Protect her beautiful
Yet tattered heart
From the cruel past that haunts her shadows
But transformed her into a warrior
Repair her tortured soul form her disastrous mind
And watch her ignite into gold.

Mend Your Garden

Misery made me learn
That misfortune can grow roots in new soil
Can enlighten burnt-out embers in my soul

Pain taught me
That flowers can survive being trampled on
And drowned in storms
So, no matter how hard it pours
My flower will rise from its roots
Maybe not now
Maybe not for another 5 years
But when it blooms
It will be the most
Beautiful fucking flower in the garden
Because pain nourished it to grow.

Sleep On It

She was tired
Tired of the anguish
Tired of not being good enough
Tired of giving more
To someone who did not deserve her
So she wept
And slept
And when she woke, she used the pain to motivate
A change
She grew into a beautiful broken soul
Who was worth so much
Even in such a little world.

Let Her Revive You

Drink her skin
Feel the warmth of her breath on your lungs
Let her revive your defeated soul
Allow her to mend your tainted pieces
And salvage your admirable heart
From the mountain of debris.

A Work Of Art

Your body
Is the canvas
Your heart
The paint
Your mind
The brush
And you
The masterpiece.

Honey & Ash

Have you ever seen those girls
Carved from ash and honey?
Their hearts dance across their skin
Their smiles melt all of your sins
Ash falls like stardust from their tongues
Raw and young
Power seeps from their lips
Leaving a taste of remarkable confidence
Have you ever looked at those girls
Wondering what it felt like
To be made of gold and never having to wonder
Am I good enough?
Maybe one day
I will allow the rain to melt my glass heart
And honey will drip from my pores
And I will become
One of those girls carved from
Honey and ash.

Poetry Is Her

She breathes oceans into sandboxes
Carves her skin with antidotes to repair you
Red scars line her flesh
Bleeding struggles onto paper
She binds poetry in light and growth
Because pieces of her are not pretty
She would rather mesmerize you
With the galaxy she creates
Than display the raw fragments that tie her together
So she scrapes poetry into her skin
And will make you believe that she is whole.

07.22

Stop letting the dagger of another's words
Lacerate the way you view yourself.

Beautiful Heart Filled With Bruises

Abuse is not love
And I am so sorry
No one has ever shown you the kind of love
You truly deserve.

Receive What You Give Out

We must make those who feel unworthy
Feel worthy
And worship the ones
Who worships us.

We Are One

If you ever lose your wings
And forget how to fly
Take the rest of mine
And I will teach you how to rise.

Help Her Transform

Flowers intertwined in her heart
Sprouting petals between her lungs
Weeds trying to grow amongst the soil
She is fragile
Yet she still grows
Shower her with patience
And watch her transform.

Regrowth

Sometimes you have to struggle through a tragedy
A heartbreak
(or four different ones)
Nights of tears drowning your feelings
Days of wanting to drink the memories away
But one day
You will wake up
And there will be no tears left to cry
Your heart will continue to beat
And you will breathe your first breath of prosperity.

Freedom

While the moon dances with darkness
I will drink the stars
And frolic amongst the summer's air.

You Matter

It is all a deception
That the air we inhale is unique
That the ground we walk upon belongs to only one
This is our home
We all belong
Together as one.

You Deserve The World And So Much More

She realized what feelings and actions she earned
And more importantly
Who deserved her delicate heart
And she was never going to accept anything less.

You Are Made Of Diamonds Darling

Drink up your self-worth
Bathe in self-security
Quench your skin in the love of yourself
Engrave the good residing within your skeleton
Because you dictate your self-worth
And darling
I know your bones exude gold
Your flesh is stitched with infatuation
Your heart beats fiercely
To a rhythm that echoes power
You are worth every fragment of love out there
Now it's your turn to see everything
That I see in you.

Together We Stand, Together We Fall

Blood in the sky
Smoke in our lungs
We will scream until the clouds
Are filled with our voices
We will howl the message that their lives matter
Because we have the privilege to breathe
When others have fallen.

Awaken

Growth is blossoming
From a seed in the depths of dark dirt
Into a Gladiolus of strength
Rising from the hollow misery
To meet the sun's delicate eminence.

Recover II

If you forgive but don't forget
Are you really forgiving
When it is still constantly on your mind?
To forgive
You should let go
And in letting go
You will grow.

Bloom

Pain changed her
Left her vain
But this agony made her realize
How to mature
How to find strength
How to love others
And life
But most importantly
How to love herself.

Admire Your Garden

If you feel like you are no one's priority
Be your own priority.

Fight Or Flight

Growth is walking into the blistering flare
Instead of turning around and running from it
Growth is throwing gasoline onto the blaze
Instead of downing the flame in rain
Growth is watching your embers turn to ash
And not being afraid to feel the burn.

Plant Your Own Garden

You are deserving of a love
That blossoms your budding flowers
Instead of drowning them in too much rain.

Chaos Wrapped In Skin

My skeleton drips
With envy
My past engraved within my bones
Drenching my lungs
With vulnerability
Forgiveness whispering
To the harp of my heart strings
This is who I am
Chaotic beauty
Love it
Or let me go.

I Deserve More

I deserve better
Than a half-assed attempt to apology

I deserve better
Than questioning whether
I am good enough for you

I deserve better
Than feeling like I did something wrong

I deserve better
Than wallowing in my anguish

I deserve better
Than giving someone multiple chances to break my heart

I deserve better than
You-
Never forget that.

Revival Of Our Words

Choke me down
Let my poetry drip down your throat
Into your heart and your soul.

PTSD

Sirens reverberate through the quilted sky
My heart beats within my windpipe
My eyes reflect the colours of fear
Years have passed
But the screeching still haunts me
And anxiety slithers
Through my spine and amongst my brain
Because when I hear the high wail of an ambulance
Near or far
I think of you
And re-live the pain.

Remembrance

Your old white sweater
Outworn, too big
Draping just above my emaciated knees
Shapeless and unrestricting
I become submerged in insubstantial fabric
Memories embedded in the seams
Tears obstructed amid the washed-out material
Ivory white that harmonized
With the colour of your porcelain skin
Smelling of your favourite lotion
And journeys yet to be traveled
Late nights and coffee stains
So when I wear your beloved sweater
I am reminded of cold nights
Your tender embrace
Your contagious laugh
Holding the thin threads together

Sewn between the stitches of that sweater
Is love that will forever last
And your memory
Suffocating me
When the collar falls against my throat

As I wear your worn-out
Faded
Ivory sweater

I am reminded of all
That this sweater has been through
All that you have been through
So I will let the fabric submerge me in retentions
And I will remember you, and I will love you
Because when I wear your favourite sweater
I am amidst you.

Safely, Locked Away

The memories danced across her sun-kissed skin
Glowing with reminiscence
That she fears will fade into the shadows
Yearning to relive
But knowing she cannot go back in time
She tucks them into the back of a locked drawer
In the base of her heart
For a time when she needs reminders
Of the occasions that vellicate within her soul.

Thunderstorm

When I was young
And the dark sapphire weighed down
On the saturated grey sky
The muted lightning
Blazed behind the blanket of my bedroom blinds
Thunder pulsing
To the same unspoken rhythm of my heart
Where the shadows came alive
Your arms would drape around my fragile body
You would count aloud
The seconds before a brilliant shock
Of white eroded the charcoal sky
With everlasting flashes of radiance
Counting to determine how distant the strikes were
You would embrace me in your adoration
Protect me from my terrors
And sing soft lullabies
Until my eyes fluttered shut
My dreams eroded away the eruption
Now as I have become an adult
The rain pounds against the concrete
The pastel blue sky
Obliterates into an aromatic rain-washed darkness
Freckled with stars
I watch as the flare rips the darkness
That hung across the sky
And count the seconds before the next

As I count
I wish more than anything you were right beside me
But mamma I know you're counting with me
Even though you are no longer with me
Counting the flickers of light that ignites the sky
Counting the seconds between each outburst
Counting the seconds until we are able to meet again.

Royalty

Your stretch marks glisten neon lights
Igniting the city that is your throne.

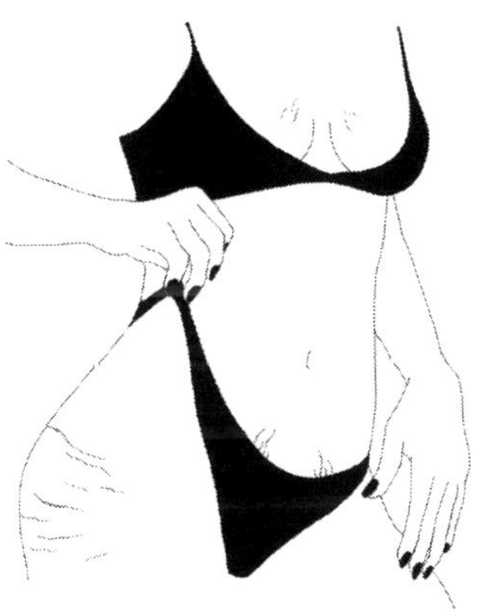

You Are Enough

Be brave enough
To love yourself-
For yourself
By yourself
And watch your seeds blossom.

Seasonal Misery

You will always get the endless possibility to grow
Because winter will always turn to spring.

She Bleeds Strength

Saturn's ring embodies her
Illuminating the strength it takes
To bleed galaxies.

Author Biography

At the age of just 22, Heather had one of her most intriguing poems, *If My Heart Were A Home,* published in the poetry collection *Broadcast,* published through Polar Express Publishing, receiving the fifth honourable mention in the *Broadcast* poetry collection that came out December 2020.

She has also graduated with honors from the Creative Writing Certificate through Stratford Career Institute, and is working towards completing the Creative Writing Certificate through the University of Calgary. Heather has been writing since the young age of 9, joining the Young Authors conference in the small town of High River, Alberta, from the ages of 10 to 16.

When Heather is not writing she is either reading, binge watching her favourite Netflix show, gaining more knowledge on the fashion industry or spending time with friends, family and her Border Collie.

You can connect with Heather through her Instagram @Heatherleighs_poetry, or her website https://heatherleighpoetry.com.

Made in the USA
Middletown, DE
21 January 2021